I Know Why the Caged Bird Sings

BARNES & NOBLE® READER'S COMPANION™
Today's take on tomorrow's classics.

FICTION
THE CORRECTIONS by Jonathan Franzen
I KNOW WHY THE CAGED BIRD SINGS by Maya Angelou
THE JOY LUCK CLUB by Amy Tan
THE LOVELY BONES by Alice Sebold
THE POISONWOOD BIBLE by Barbara Kingsolver
THE RED TENT by Anita Diamant
WE WERE THE MULVANEYS by Joyce Carol Oates
WHITE TEETH by Zadie Smith

NONFICTION
THE ART OF WAR by Sun Tzu
A BRIEF HISTORY OF TIME by Stephen Hawking
GUNS, GERMS, AND STEEL by Jared Diamond
JOHN ADAMS by David McCullough

MAYA ANGELOU'S

I Know Why the Caged Bird Sings

BARNES
&NOBLE
B O O K S

EDITORIAL DIRECTOR Justin Kestler
EXECUTIVE EDITOR Ben Florman
DIRECTOR OF TECHNOLOGY Tammy Hepps

SERIES EDITOR John Crowther
MANAGING EDITOR Vincent Janoski

WRITER Jerry Oster
EDITOR Matt Blanchard
DESIGN Dan O. Williams, Matt Daniels

This edition published by Spark Publishing

Spark Publishing
A Division of SparkNotes LLC
120 Fifth Avenue, 8th Floor
New York, NY 10011

ISBN 1-58663-864-5

Library of Congress Cataloging-in-Publication Data available upon request

Printed and bound in the United States

Contents

A TOUR OF THE BOOK   an overview of the book **1**

The Rainbow and the Razor Angelou's story is both a sensitive portrait of a childhood and a scathing indictment of race relations in America.

JOURNEYS   the characters and their stories **11**

Wandering Spirits Young Marguerite grows up in unpredictable environments shaped by a constantly changing cast of characters.

POINTS OF VIEW   a conversation about
I Know Why the Caged Bird Sings **17**

The Singer or Her Song? The sometimes searing topics Angelou explores in her memoir elicit strong opinions from the book's readers.

A WRITER'S LIFE   Maya Angelou's story **43**

A Golden Voice Angelou has an unequaled place in American culture—a giant in letters, poetry, civil rights, feminism, and oratory.

THE WORLD OUTSIDE   a look at Angelou's 1930s America **47**

Red, White, Black, and Blue Angelou's early life plays out amid the slew of social and economic hardships America faced in the mid-twentieth century.

A BRIEF HISTORY   the critics respond to
I Know Wny the Caged Bird Sings **53**

Breaking New Ground *I Know Why the Caged Bird Sings* marked a new era in memoir, African-American writing, and women's writing.

EXPLORE   books to consider reading next **57**

Other Books of Interest Angelou's memoir was a pioneering work for countless other African-American and women writers.

BARNES & NOBLE® READER'S COMPANION™

WITH INTELLIGENT CONVERSATION AND ENGAGING
commentary from a variety of perspectives, BARNES & NOBLE READER'S COMPANIONS are the perfect complement to today's most widely read and discussed books.

Whether you're reading on your own or as part of a book club, BARNES & NOBLE READER'S COMPANIONS provide insights and perspectives on today's most interesting reads: What are other people saying about this book? What's the author trying to tell me?

Pick up the BARNES & NOBLE READER'S COMPANION to learn more about what you're reading. From the big picture down to the details, you'll get today's take on tomorrow's classics.

I Know Why the Caged Bird Sings

The Rainbow and the Razor

Angelou's story is both a sensitive portrait of a childhood and a scathing indictment of race relations in America.

○ ○ ○

MAYA ANGELOU'S *I KNOW WHY THE CAGED BIRD SINGS* is so vivid and powerful a work that it remains in print more than thirty years after its publication. It continues to move readers—and to outrage those who have never read it but would nevertheless ban it from schools and public libraries. Its indelible descriptions of poverty, racism, and sexual abuse are all the more shocking and poignant because they are the products not of a novelist's imagination but of a memoirist's real, lived experience.

The work is effectively the first chapter of a six-part autobiography, the final installment of which was published in 2002. *I Know Why the Caged Bird Sings* was a landmark book in a number of genres—autobiography, African-American history, Depression history, feminist memoir, abuse-victim case study. Angelou's frank and explicit description of her shattered childhood stands alongside such classics of self-examination as Richard Wright's *Black Boy*, James Baldwin's *Nobody Knows My Name*, and Eldridge Cleaver's *Soul on Ice*. Modern black writers like Toni Morrison, Ishmael Reed, Bebe Moore Campbell, Terry McMillan, and E. Lynn Harris stand on Maya Angelou's shoulders.

I Know Why the Caged Bird Sings launched a career that is nearly without parallel: Angelou is not only a bestselling and respected writer, but also a prominent poet, screenwriter, actress, teacher, and leader of the civil rights and feminist movements. She is simultaneously one of America's best-known African-American women, best-known African Americans, and best-known women.

1

INTRODUCTION AND CHAPTERS 1–7
MARGUERITE IN STAMPS

A girl named Marguerite is the first-person narrator of *I Know Why the Caged Bird Sings*, but her tone of voice and observations are not at all childlike. The book opens with a comical moment of childhood embarrassment, as Marguerite struggles to remember the words of a poem in front of a Sunday school class and struggles at the same time to control her bladder. The anecdote creates a tension that persists throughout the book. We are unsure where we are in time and space, unsure what to make of Marguerite. She describes herself humorously, as a big, ungainly black girl in a white woman's hand-me-down dress. She confides her fantasy that an evil stepmother has transformed her from her real self, a blond, blue-eyed Caucasian. But Marguerite ends the opening chapter with a violent image that surprises and jars: "If growing up is painful for the Southern Black girl, being aware of her displacement is the rust on the razor that threatens the throat."

Angelou quickly establishes that Marguerite is no ordinary child. She views the world with a premature sophistication. Her family migrated to California, seeking the promise of new jobs and new lives. But the Depression held the nation in its grip, and when Marguerite was three and her brother, Bailey, four, their parents tied tags on their wrists and put them on a train bound for tiny Stamps, Arkansas, and the care of their paternal grandmother, Annie Henderson.

Reading Angelou's descriptions of the life in Stamps reminds us of other classics of American poverty, such as John Steinbeck's *The Grapes of Wrath* or James Agee's *Let Us Now Praise Famous Men*. Annie Henderson—her neighbors call her Sister Henderson, her grandchildren call her Momma—seems like a character straight out of fiction. A natural entrepreneur, she built the Wm. Johnson General Merchandise Store in the heart of Stamps's black community. "The Store," as it's known, sells everything, from animal feed and hair tonic to onions, oranges, and chewing tobacco. The Store is also a community center, a temporary shop for roving barbers, and a weekend stage for blues singers and cigar-box guitarists.

Angelou's narrative contains striking contrasts on nearly every page. Although poverty and racism circumscribe Marguerite's and Bailey's lives, the children are avid learners nonetheless. Their Uncle Willie, crippled as a child when a babysitter dropped him, drills them on their multiplication tables by threatening to hold their hands to a potbellied stove when they make mistakes. Marguerite reads Shakespeare, Kipling, Poe, and Thackeray, although she knows Momma doesn't approve of white writers—not even dead ones. Marguerite reads pioneering African-American writers too: Paul Lawrence Dunbar, Langston Hughes, and W.E.B. Du Bois.

But if the Store and black Stamps are safe havens, white Stamps is another matter, a place of dread, occupied by pale aliens with small feet and strange walks. When a lynch mob searches for a black man suspected of molesting a white woman, Sister Henderson and the children hide Uncle Willie in a storage bin in the Store, covering him with potatoes and onions. Even stranger than white folks are "powhitetrash," some of whom live on Sister Henderson's land. In an extraordinary vignette, Mar-

> *"People were those who lived on my side of town. . . . These others, the strange pale creatures that lived in their alien unlife, weren't considered folks. They were whitefolks."*

guerite watches three powhitetrash girls try—and fail—to humiliate her grandmother, who puts herself into a kind of trance, humming a spiritual hymn and steadfastly refusing to acknowledge the girls' indignities.

There are scenes in Angelou's memoir that read like chapters from a great comic novel. Like the book's opening scene, some of them take place in the Colored Methodist Episcopal Church. Services are enlivened by parishioners like Sister Monroe, who is fond of shouting "Preach it!" to the presiding minister. She tackles one reverend with such fervor that she knocks the false teeth out of his mouth.

CHAPTERS 8–13
RITIE IN ST. LOUIS

I Know Why the Caged Bird Sings moves without warning from the general to the pointedly particular, from humor to pathos, from childlike observations to preternatural wisdom—all within a few pages, sometimes just a few paragraphs. Marguerite's sardonic description of racism in Stamps slides into a prim lecture on the wastefulness of white people, then to a grim catalogue of the economic realities of the Depression, and finally to the stunning revelation that Marguerite and Bailey believe their parents are not really in California, but are dead. Christmas presents—a tea set and a blond, blue-eyed doll (like Marguerite's fantasy of her true self)—only raise more questions and increase the children's feelings of abandonment.

> *"To describe my mother would be to write about a hurricane in its perfect power. Or the climbing, falling colors of a rainbow."*

The frequent arrival of strange men introduces a sense of menace and uncertainty to Angelou's memoir. The first is the children's father, Bailey Sr., who shows up driving a big De Soto, wearing a suit too small for his large frame, and speaking an accented English that makes Marguerite wonder if he is actually a brown-skinned white man. Without discussion, Bailey Sr. takes the children to St. Louis, their mother's hometown, and then abruptly returns to California, still a stranger to his offspring.

Angelou's frenetic portrait of Prohibition-era St. Louis shoves aside our memory of the peaceful, sleepy town of Stamps. St. Louis is a city with a gold-rush, wild-west atmosphere, resounding with such strange sounds as flushing toilets and ringing doorbells. It is peopled by the likes of the children's Grandmother Baxter, who looks white and speaks with the accent of the German family that raised her, and her three sons, who are notoriously fond of fighting. The children's mother, Vivian Baxter Johnson, a stunning beauty known as Bibbie, spends much of her time at a tavern where she dances and sings blues. Although trained as a nurse, Bibbie decides to live on the financial support of her boyfriend, Mr. Freeman. A railroad foreman, Mr. Freeman is yet another ominous male presence, a soft, mysterious man who hardly speaks to the children, never reads a newspaper or listens to the radio, and devotes himself to waiting for the beautiful Bibbie to come home.

Almost imperceptibly, *I Know Why the Caged Bird Sings* becomes a horror story that is all the more powerful because the voice of eight-year old Marguerite—whom the family now calls Ritie—remains relentlessly candid. Overwhelmed by the foreignness of St. Louis, a place she refuses to think of as a new home, she suffers from recurring nightmares. To comfort Ritie, Bibbie takes her into her bed, along with Mr. Freeman. One morning, after Bibbie has gone out on an errand, Mr. Freeman embraces Ritie in bed and masturbates alongside her. Our shock at this disgusting act grows deeper when we read Ritie's reaction, ". . . then came the nice part. He held me so softly that I wished he wouldn't ever let me go." Perhaps this man was her real father, a potential source of the comfort she has long been seeking.

Matter-of-factly, with remarkable detail, unnerving artistry, and even wit, Ritie then describes the late spring Saturday when Mr. Freeman rapes her in the living room of their mother's house. Bibbie had not come home the night before, and although Ritie never says so explicitly, we are left to conclude that Mr. Freeman's assault is an act of revenge by a cuckolded lover. The power of the scene is augmented by Ritie's attempts to behave normally—putting on her underwear, looking for her brother (whom Mr. Freeman threatens to kill if she ever tells anyone), watching some boys play baseball, counting the cracks in the sidewalk, hiding her bloodstained underwear under her mattress, getting into bed in the middle of the afternoon. The catalogue of normalcy is overwhelming: Bibbie administers chicken broth, thinking Ritie just has the measles; Bailey reads to Ritie from an adventure novel; Bailey and Bibbie change the sheets on Ritie's bed and discover her hidden underwear.

We are left exhausted, though relieved that the assault is discovered, freeing Ritie from the burden of keeping her secret any longer. But the ordeal isn't over. Testifying at Mr. Freeman's trial, Ritie realizes she must lie and say that he never molested her prior to the rape, lest she appear to have encouraged his advances. Convicted, sentenced to a year in jail, and released on a legal technicality all in the space of twenty-four hours, Freeman is then beaten to death by unknown assailants. By Bibbie's belligerent brothers? Angelou doesn't say, but we can't help but draw that conclusion. Ritie is horrified that a man has died, even one who assaulted her. She blames herself for Freeman's death and vows to stop speaking.

CHAPTERS 14–24
BACK TO STAMPS

Having painstakingly and painfully detailed Ritie's rape, Angelou is notably terse about her silence, which lasts nearly a year. Sent back to Stamps and their grandmother, the children are local celebrities because of their travels to the north. Bailey regales anyone who will listen with tales—rather tall tales—of flush toilets, skyscrapers, iceboxes, and snow. People assume that Ritie, now known as Marguerite again, is pining for the big city, and they regard her speechlessness as a sign of sensitivity, not stubbornness—and certainly not trauma. A friend of Momma's, the aristocratic and intellectual Bertha Flowers, takes an interest in Marguerite. She serves Marguerite lemonade and cookies, reads to her from her favorite book, A *Tale of Two Cities*, and gently coaxes the girl to break her silence.

> **After years of tragically premature maturity, Marguerite finally becomes a child.**

Mirroring the fact that Marguerite's life has achieved a kind of normalcy, Angelou's narrative becomes less intense, more discursive: memories of Saturdays in Stamps; a curious anecdote about Bailey's thinking the white actress Kay Francis is actually his mother; a vivid account of a tent revival meeting; an exciting account of the crowd jammed into the Store to listen to a radio broadcast of a championship fight between Primo Carnera and Joe Louis; and the summer picnic fish fry with music, dancing, food, and flirtation.

After years of tragically premature maturity, Marguerite finally becomes a child. She makes her first female friend, Louise. She receives her first valentine, which causes both pleasure and consternation because she knows that love is connected with sex, which has only dark associations for her. Marguerite never tells Louise about the rape that occurred in St. Louis—a nightmare that "hadn't really happened to me. It happened to a nasty little girl, years and years before, who had no chain on me at all."

But Marguerite cannot put her past entirely behind her. Memories of St. Louis intrude even on her graduation from eighth grade, a significant event in the life of a poor black child. Marguerite is near the top of her class, and though she is only twelve, she knows that she has as much education as many black teachers in Arkansas. But in the back of her mind is a sense that she might never have lived to see this day. And Angelou never lets us forget the unrelenting misery of the lives of poor black people in her day. A white graduation speaker insults the students by suggesting that they can only become athletes or workers. A white dentist says he would rather put his hand in a dog's mouth than in Marguerite's. Bailey witnesses the discovery of the body of a drowned black man—and the gleeful grin of one of the white men who retrieves the bloated corpse. Momma decides it's time to take the children to California, first to Los Angeles, where their father lives, and then to San Francisco to see their mother.

CHAPTERS 25–36
MAYA IN CALIFORNIA

Angelou again abruptly disorients us with a new set of images. This time, visions of life in California—a foreign place with white landlords, Mexican neighbors, streets with Spanish names, and supermarkets that seem larger than the entire town of Stamps. We feel uneasy at the return of the charismatic Bibbie. Now called Vivian, she is still beautiful, still captivating, driving a big car with one hand while smoking a cigarette with the other, waking the children in the middle of the night for a party of biscuits and hot chocolate, dancing the Time Step for them, the Snake Hips, and the Suzy Q.

Vivian is proud that she isn't a servant, that she instead works at a couple of Oakland saloons, running pinochle or poker games and flirting with customers. She recently shot and wounded a man, a partner in a gambling casino—an incident that Angelou rationalizes as the result of her mother's passionate nature. Shortly after her children arrive, just weeks before the Japanese attack on Pearl Harbor, Vivian marries a businessman known as Daddy Clidell, yet another of the mysterious males in this narrative.

Once again, we begin to feel a sense of dread below the chatty surface of the narrative. On a quick trip to Mexico, the thirteen-year-old Marguerite—who for the first time is called Maya, a name derived from Bailey's babyhood reference to her as "Mya sister"—sees another side of her natural father. The womanizing Bailey Sr. passes out drunk, forcing Maya to drive a car for the first time in order to get them back across the U.S. border. Bailey's current girlfriend, outraged at his long absence, blames Maya for his departure and stabs her in the side with a claw hammer.

> *"The fact that the American Negro female emerges a formidable character is often met with amazement, distaste and even belligerence."*

The few pages that follow the stabbing are among the most extraordinary in the book, and the most cryptic. Once again, Maya blames herself for someone else's violent behavior. Afraid to go back to her mother, she runs away from Bailey's house and joins a street gang of black, Mexican, and white children in Los Angeles. Maya spends a month with the gang, whose members share the money they earn collecting bottles and doing odd jobs. Maya learns to drive, to curse, and to dance the jitterbug. Remarkably, she also experiences, for the first time, unquestioning acceptance and the end of her lifelong insecurity: "I was never again to sense myself so solidly outside the pale of the human race. The lack of criticism evidenced by our ad hoc community influenced me, and set a tone of tolerance for my life."

Finally back in San Francisco, Maya finds Vivian and Bailey Jr. at war over Bailey's new fondness for zoot suits, sloe gin, and white prostitutes. Though only sixteen, Bailey leaves home for a shabby rooming house and, eventually, for the merchant marine. Maya too strikes out for new territory, persisting against racism and bureaucratic obstacles to win a job as a San Francisco streetcar conductor, the first black conductor in the city. Returning to school in the spring, she realizes—as we have realized chapters earlier—that she has changed inalterably: "I had gone from being ignorant of being ignorant to being aware of being aware." Aware of what, though, Maya is still not sure.

It comes as no surprise to us that one subject about which Maya is both aware *and* ignorant is sexuality. Her reading—*The Well of Loneliness* by Radclyffe Hall—has introduced her to lesbianism, which she mistakes for hermaphroditism. Otherwise, she is woefully ignorant about the development of her body. She determines that she needs a boyfriend to "clarify my position to the world and, even more important, to myself," so she selects as her target a handsome neighbor. They have intercourse once, awkwardly, swiftly, silently. Three weeks later, the sixteen-year old Maya discovers that she's pregnant. She blames herself, of course, though this time she recognizes that she in fact *is* partly responsible.

The last few pages of *I Know Why the Caged Bird Sings* have a tragic offhandedness about them. We are aware that Maya is more alone than she has been at any time in her life. Bailey is off at sea, Momma is far away in Stamps, Vivian is in Alaska overseeing the opening of a night-club, Daddy Clidell is focused on his businesses. Approximately eight months pregnant, on the night of her graduation from high school, Maya finally reveals her condition to her parents.

Three weeks later, Maya has a baby boy—"totally mine." Totally hers, and yet she is afraid to touch him, afraid of crushing him in her sleep. Three weeks go by before she gives in to Vivian's insistence that she take the baby into bed with her. Maya falls asleep and wakes to find the baby safely tucked against her. Vivian whispers to her: "See, you don't have to

> ## "I know what the caged bird feels . . ."
>
> The title of *I Know Why the Caged Bird Sings* was taken from the poem "Sympathy" (1899) by Paul Laurence Dunbar (1872–1906), an African-American poet and novelist who influenced many twentieth-century black writers. Dunbar wrote the poem while working as an assistant at the Library of Congress, and some scholars believe the library's metal stacks reminded him of the bars of a birdcage.

think about doing the right thing. If you're for the right thing, then you do it without thinking."

On reaching the end of *I Know Why the Caged Bird Sings*, we realize that Angelou has never explained the title. A note on the copyright page acknowledges that it is taken from a poem, "Sympathy," by Paul Laurence Dunbar, one of the black writers the young Ritie admired. The poem, published in 1899, is a wrenching lament that begins, "I know what the caged bird feels, alas!" and contains images of an imprisoned bird beating its wings until they are bloody and broken. The song the bird sings "is not a carol of joy or glee," but a prayer, "a plea, that upward to Heaven he flings." Maya Angelou's Marguerite-Ritie-Maya, though still woefully inexperienced, has succeeded in prying apart the bars of her cage, and can at least glimpse freedom. Her song, if not one of triumph, is at least a signal that she survives.

Wandering Spirits

Young Marguerite grows up in unpredictable environments shaped by a constantly changing cast of characters.

○ ○ ○

MARGUERITE / RITIE / MAYA JOHNSON

Also occasionally known as Sister, Mary, and My, the narrator of *I Know Why the Caged Bird Sings* is a girl forced too soon to be a woman. Her wrenching real-life experiences have a stranger-than-fiction quality. There are three major dramatic arcs in Marguerite's story: her years in rural Stamps, under the loving if strict influence of her paternal grandmother, Annie Henderson; her life in cosmopolitan, frenetic St. Louis with her charismatic but erratic mother, a time marred by her sexual abuse and rape at the hands of her mother's boyfriend; and her return to Stamps and then to California, a period highlighted by her increasing independence, her first job, and her pregnancy.

Marguerite first sees herself as an awkward African-American child in a world dominated by whites. Although she gains self-confidence as she grows older, she is so devastated by her rape that she blames herself for the community's revenge killing of the rapist and deliberately refuses to talk for nearly a year. Marguerite's experiences in California contribute to a growing sense of self-worth, but the rather matter-of-fact way in which she becomes pregnant points to the quintessential need she feels to love and be loved—a need she is mostly unable to fulfill.

Women are the anchors of Marguerite's life: her grandmothers; her first friend, Louise; the aristocratic Bertha Flowers; even her mercurial mother. The men in her world are unpredictable, unreliable, cruel, and fearsome. Her father, her mother's many boyfriends, the father of her own child—all are disruptive forces in Marguerite's life. Even her beloved brother, Bailey Jr., ultimately disappoints her, leaving home first to live with a white prostitute and then to join the merchant marine.

BAILEY JOHNSON, JR.

Known as Junior or simply Ju, Bailey is Marguerite's senior by one year, her playmate, partner in learning, advisor, and protector. Bailey is his mother's son—beautiful, charming, beguiling, and so popular in Stamps that it takes him hours to do a simple errand because he has to stop and talk to so many people. Bailey is more loving toward and protective of his sister than any of the adult males in the memoir. There is almost no discussion of Bailey's relationship to his father or to the various father figures with whom he comes in contact. (Although it is striking that Bailey affects an English accent, an echo of his father's accent, which Marguerite thinks sounds white.) But Bailey's tender care of Marguerite after her assault by Mr. Freeman establishes himself as a father figure in his own right. When he learns of Marguerite's pregnancy, Bailey advises against telling their mother and counsels Marguerite to finish school and get her diploma. There is a tragic quality to Bailey, especially in his estrangement from his mother, who never returns in kind his extraordinary love for her. He wants so desperately for Vivian to love him that he goes so far as to try to become just like the men she loves. In his relationship with a white prostitute, Bailey exactly parallels Mr. Freeman's relationship with Vivian.

> There is a **tragic** quality to Bailey, especially in his **estrangement** from his **mother,** who never **returns** in **kind** his **extraordinary love** for her.

ANNIE HENDERSON

"Sister Henderson" to her neighbors and customers at the Store in Stamps, "Momma" to her grandchildren, Annie Henderson is a remarkably resourceful woman. In her capacity as the economic hub of the black community of Stamps, she is also a moral and religious center. She is a model to her grandchildren for maintaining an enduring dignity despite the humiliations and dangers of her racist surroundings. Momma's decision to move her grandchildren to California—a choice she makes after Bailey Jr.'s traumatizing encounter with the corpse of a drowned black man—is sketched only off-handedly in the book. But by making up her mind to reunite her grandchildren with their parents, Momma takes a step that almost certainly leads to Marguerite Johnson's transformation into Maya Angelou, her transformation from a girl from Stamps into a woman of the world.

VIVIAN BAXTER JOHNSON

A trained nurse who makes a living working in nightclubs, a mother who lives apart from her children, a wife whose husband lives in a different city, a lover who teases her boyfriend by staying out late in the company of other men, Vivian is the most charismatic and most fickle character in Angelou's narrative. Marguerite excuses much of her mother's behavior by attributing it to her extraordinary beauty.

But Vivian's beauty is also destructive. We sense that her staying out late and going off early contributes somewhat to the sexual and emotional frustration that culminates in Mr. Freeman's rape of Marguerite. It is Bailey, not Vivian, who cries upon learning of the assault of his sister. Vivian brings flowers and candy to Marguerite's hospital bed, but if she says any words of consolation to her daughter, they are not recorded in these pages. The one clear action Vivian does take is to send her children back to their grandmother's in Arkansas—an action that devastates her son, though Vivian doesn't seem to notice.

Even when the children return to live with her in San Francisco, Vivian doesn't make them the focus of her life. There is always a man to spend time with, a full house to entertain at a nightclub, a business venture to explore. Vivian's failure to teach Maya about sex leads to her daughter's early pregnancy. Vivian's final words to Maya about "doing the right thing" in raising her new baby have a hollow ring to them, for Vivian has so often chosen, in raising her own children, to do nothing at all.

BAILEY JOHNSON, SR.

An absentee father whose idea of an appropriate Christmas present for his daughter is a photograph of himself, Bailey Sr. is fond of showy cars, grand entrances, and beautiful women. Big, handsome, and flashy, he affects an accent that makes Marguerite wonder momentarily if he is the world's only brown-skinned white man. Angelou's first description of him—"He was the first cynic I had met"—is devastating, and nothing he ever does overcomes her mistrust and suspicion of him. There is a desperate quality to Bailey Sr.'s interactions with the world, especially during the so-called vacation he takes to Mexico with Marguerite. Her last mention of her father in the book is poignant, for it reveals the depth of his insincerity: ". . . he asked how I felt, gave me a dollar and a half and a kiss, and said he'd drop by late in the evening. He laughed as usual. Nervous?"

MR. FREEMAN

Vivian's boyfriend and her daughter's rapist, Mr. Freeman is a terrifying figure—all the more so because he is so helpless and seemingly innocuous. He works the day shift as a railroad yard foreman and gets home from work after Vivian has gone out for the evening. He eats the dinner Vivian has prepared for him and then waits for her to come home—waits inexorably, never reading or listening to the radio or talking to the children. Vivian's return animates Freeman, and she sits on his lap or dances *for* him— never *with* him. A big, bear-like man, Freeman reminds Ritie of a pig being fattened for slaughter. He exacerbates his sexual abuse of Ritie with the psychological abuse he inflicts to cover up his deeds. He tells Ritie that the semen on the bed sheets after he masturbates is actually her fault— that she wet the bed. He warns her over and over that he'll kill Bailey if she says even a word about what happened. Before the rape, Freeman warns her even more strongly that he'll kill Bailey if she screams or tells. He repeats the warning while Vivian and Bailey are caring for Ritie, thinking that she has a fever. Freeman's last words to Ritie, the last words he speaks in the book, are "If you tell . . . If you tell." During his trial, Freeman looks threateningly at Ritie, but she is confident that Bailey will be safe. The last we see of Freeman in the memoir is his stare across the courtroom at Ritie, who is about to tell the lie she must tell to save her self-respect.

UNCLE WILLIE JOHNSON

Bailey Sr.'s younger brother, Uncle Willie has lived all his life with his mother, Momma Henderson. Dropped by a baby-sitter as a toddler, Willie is disabled, so that when he sits, he looks to the children like "a giant black Z." In a moving anecdote early in the memoir, Marguerite describes how Uncle Willie hides his infirmity from a couple of strangers by pretending to be standing upright behind a counter in the Store when he is actually supporting himself with great effort on his arms and hands. Marguerite speculates that Willie suddenly became tired of being disabled, just as prisoners tire of prison bars and "the guilty tire of blame" — a metaphor that foreshadows Ritie's later struggles with guilt over the lie she tells about Mr. Freeman.

On the whole, however, Willie is not as weak a figure as we might expect. He endures jokes that those who are less well off and less gainfully employed make at his expense. He is his mother's son as far as discipline is concerned. He threatens his niece and nephew with a hot stove if they don't learn their multiplication tables and he administers a whipping when the children can't restrain themselves from laughing in church at the overenthusiastic Sister Monroe. The children learn about racism through Uncle Willie, as they help their grandmother hide him in a storage bin on a night when the Ku Klux Klan is riding. When the children return to Stamps after Marguerite's rape, Marguerite wonders if Uncle Willie knows what happened to her. She doesn't want "a cripple's sympathy" because she feels crippled herself. Nor does she want him to think of her as a sinner. Willie barely appears in the narrative after that, and we wonder how he fares when his mother is in California for six months with the children. The final mention of Willie is the explanation that Momma must leave California because "she was needed by Uncle Willie."

DADDY CLIDELL

Vivian's second husband, Clidell is a businessman whom Ritie expects to be just another faceless conquest of Vivian's, but who turns out to be "the first father I would know." An uneducated owner of apartment buildings and pool halls, Clidell is a simple, decent man, famous among his peers for being a "man of honor." His contribution to Ritie's and Bailey's upbringing is teaching them how to play poker, blackjack, and other card games and introducing them to his colorful con-man friends. Unaware that Marguerite is pregnant, Vivian goes off to Alaska to open a night-club, leaving her daughter in the care of Daddy Clidell. It is one of the few times in the memoir that we feel comfortable knowing that Marguerite is around a responsible adult male.

MRS. BERTHA FLOWERS

Marguerite tells us that Mrs. Flowers is "the aristocrat of Black Stamps," though she never explains precisely what that means. Mrs. Flowers is thin, graceful, and benign. She looks cool on the hottest days, and—an extraordinary statement—"has remained throughout my life the measure of what a human being can be." During Marguerite's silent period, Mrs. Flowers one day asks that the girl help her carry home some groceries she's bought at the store. Mrs. Flowers casually remarks that no one can make Marguerite talk, but that the ability to talk is what separates mankind from the animals. Just reading words on the page, she says, is not enough—a human voice must read words out loud to "infuse them with the shades of deeper meaning." Mrs. Flowers serves Marguerite cookies and lemonade and gives her some "lessons in living," teaching the girl that even uneducated, illiterate people can be possessed of great natural wit and wisdom. Mrs. Flowers reads to Marguerite from Dickens's *A Tale of Two Cities* and gives her a book of poetry, telling her she expects her to recite a poem from memory the next time she visits. Mrs. Flowers's friendship has a transforming effect: for the first time, Marguerite feels liked and respected—not for being her grandmother's grandchild or her brother's sister, but for being herself.

> **Mrs. Flowers' friendship** has a **transforming effect:** for the **first** time, **Marguerite** feels **liked** and **respected.**

The Singer or Her Song?

The sometimes searing topics Angelou explores in her memoir elicit strong opinions from the book's readers.

○　○　○

Some critics complain that *Caged Bird* is angry and accusatory, that Angelou makes little attempt to promote understanding across races. Is this a valid criticism?

"YES, ANGELOU'S ANGER IS PRESENT IN THE BOOK. SHE OFFERS FEW SOLUTIONS TO RACIAL PROBLEMS."

Marguerite's first striking metaphor is an angry and disturbing one, an image of the rust on the razor that threatens the throat of young black women in the South. Near the end of the novel, Angelou observes that adult black women are assaulted by the forces of "masculine prejudice, white illogical hate, and Black lack of power." In between, she pulls no punches in her mistrust of and contempt for whites. The few white people in the book are barely even characters. They are either evil or criminally ignorant. A white reader in search of empathy, for constructive solutions to America's racial problems, isn't going to find them here.

"ANGELOU IS ANGRY, BUT SHE MEANS TO RETELL AN EXPERIENCE, NOT TO PROVIDE ANSWERS."

Angelou means her memoir to be just that—a record of her experience as a young black woman in the South in the first half of the twentieth century. She tells us with great candor and honesty about all of the major emotions she experienced as a child—loneliness, confusion, love, and anger, among many others. From that foundation we must form our own responses. We empathize with much of what Angelou says, feel shock at some of it, and perhaps disagree with some of it. But the point of a memoir is to present an experience honestly for others to interpret, react to, think about, and discuss. It's not fair to accuse Angelou of failing to explicitly reach out to other races or offer solutions if that's not her intention. In a sense, by recording and communicating her experience she's reaching out—after all, anyone, white, black, or otherwise, can read her book if they choose and take whatever conclusions and insights they want from it.

○ ○ ○

Angelou's memoir is one of the most widely banned books in American history. Why?

"THE BOOK IS VERY FRANK ABOUT SEX, AND IT BROKE MANY TABOOS WHEN IT WAS PUBLISHED MORE THAN THIRTY YEARS AGO."

Marguerite describes her rape explicitly, vividly, and unforgettably. Her vocabulary is largely that of a child with only a vague understanding of sex and of her own body. Mr. Freeman's penis is his "mushy-hard thing." Marguerite doesn't describe her own genitalia at all, except in the extraordinary metaphor of "the needle giving because the camel can't." Afterwards, she thinks she has wet the bed and feels as though her hips are dislocated. The images are shocking, unnerving, nearly overwhelming. Marguerite was eight years old, we should not forget. To describe these images as lewd or pornographic is to raise the inconceivable possibility that Angelou ever intended them to arouse or titillate—which is ridiculous.

"THERE HAVE ALSO BEEN OBJECTIONS THAT THE BOOK IS SACRILEGIOUS."

Many of the book's comic moments take place in church: Marguerite's consternation at forgetting the poem in the opening chapter, the overly enthusiastic Sister Monroe, the tent revival meeting. All are vivid—and vividly secular—moments. To assert that they are antireligious is to overlook the essential humanity of the people involved. Angelou never mocks these people; she simply describes them. She is far from devout, but she isn't impious either. She never curses God for the awful things that happen to her. For Angelou and her African-American community, people who went to church were people who "had forsaken their own distress for a little while."

"*CAGED BIRD* IS TARGETED FOR SUCH HARSH CRITICISM SIMPLY BECAUSE IT'S THE PERSONAL HISTORY OF AN AFRICAN-AMERICAN WOMAN."

In *Understanding I Know Why the Caged Bird Sings* (1998), Joanne Megna-Wallace cites a 1996 report showing that critical and censorship attacks have singled out "a disproportionate number of books written by African-American women." The report suggests that these attacks are part of a broader challenge to multicultural education, an attempt to block "efforts to make history and English curricula more accurate and complete by including contributions of women and minorities." Groups from the religious right are behind a number of the censorship efforts of Angelou's work. Their most frequent complaint has been that the book is offensive in its treatment of sexuality, but they have also raised objections to its language and to its perceived religious beliefs.

Caged Bird broke new ground as a memoir in that it was both a critical and popular success. Why might that be the case?

"IT'S A GREAT STORY TOLD IN AN HONEST, ENGAGING, COLLOQUIAL VOICE."

From Marguerite's first self-deprecating description of herself, it's clear that this is no ordinary account of growing up poor, black, and female. She's honest enough to make herself look awkward, and there's something appealing about that kind of honesty. As we get further into her story, and particularly as she experiences tragedy, we're compelled to read on just as we're motivated by the very best fiction.

"IT'S A NEW VOICE BECAUSE IT'S A WOMAN'S STORY, THE FIRST BESTSELLING MEMOIR BY AN AFRICAN-AMERICAN WOMAN."

From first to last—from feeling foolish in a hand-me-down dress to being sexually abused to giving birth—*I Know Why the Caged Bird Sings* never lets us forget that it's what some people call "herstory" rather than merely history. The women in the memoir—Marguerite / Ritie / Maya, Sister Annie Henderson, Louise Kendricks, Grandmother Baxter, Vivian Baxter Johnson, Bertha Flowers—are all much more vivid than the men. Uncle Willie, Bailey Sr., Daddy Clidell, even Angelou's beloved brother, Bailey Jr., are often sketched in just a few words or phrases. Only the horrific Mr. Freeman is a full-blown portrait on the scale of the portraits of the women in the book. And for good reason: he is at one and the same time the most real male, and also the most inhuman. He requires a full-fledged portrait if we are to understand his flawed nature. But on the whole, Angelou's book broke ground because it presents the voice of an African-American woman, a new voice that hadn't been heard in memoirs before its time.

"IT WAS AMONG THE FIRST OF ITS KIND IN SEVERAL DIFFERENT GENRES."

We tend to think of *I Know Why the Caged Bird Sings* as part of a tradition of memoir writing that includes recent books like *Drinking: A Love Story*,

Caroline Knapp's memoir of alcoholism, or the incest memoirs *The Kiss* by Kathryn Harrison and *The Architect of Desire* by Suzannah Lessard. But we have to remember that the *Caged Bird* is more than thirty years old and that it was a pioneer both as a feminist document and abuse-victim document. Because it's still in print, and because Maya Angelou is such a prominent public figure, the books that are often compared to *I Know Why the Caged Bird Sings* are actually books that came long after it.

○   ○   ○

Even though *I Know Why the Caged Bird Sings* is autobiography, are we inclined to accept everything in it as true?

"NOT NECESSARILY—TRUTH IS ALWAYS AN ELUSIVE QUALITY."

In *The Silent Woman: Sylvia Plath and Ted Hughes*, Janet Malcolm notes that absolute truth exists only in fiction. When a novelist tells us that a woman loves a man, but that the man loves another woman, all those things are true. What an autobiographer tells us, what a biographer tells us, what a historian tells us are reports that are subject to interpretation, disputation, and distortion. *I Know Why the Caged Bird Sings* is autobiography and may take liberties with the truth in the best and worst of senses.

"ANGELOU IS THE FIRST TO ADMIT THAT TRUTH IS DIFFICULT TO PIN DOWN."

Angelou has been quoted in published interviews as saying that she was writing not only about her life but also about the time in which that life was lived. Many autobiographers take liberties with the facts—compressing time, creating composite characters, leaving things out—even putting things in that didn't actually happen but that best make the point the author is trying to make.

What's the significance of the different names Maya Angelou uses for herself? What associations do the different names carry?

"THE NAMES ARE A POWERFUL NARRATIVE TOOL. EACH NAME PROVIDES A DIFFERENT CONTEXT FOR ANGELOU AT A PARTICULAR POINT IN TIME."

The names, admittedly, are confusing at first. We know the book is by Maya Angelou—that's why we bought it and why we're reading it. Or even if it's not, we can see her name on the cover and on the title page. But someone else, whose name is apparently Marguerite, writes the book in the first person. We get used to that name, and then her father appears unexpectedly and doesn't call her Marguerite at all—he calls her "Daddy's baby," not once but over and over. It's terrifying. He's like a monster in a horror film. "Daddy's baby, daddy's baby, daddy's baby." There's a lot of Mr. Freeman in Bailey Sr. (though we don't know it at the time we first meet him), and his use of names for Marguerite attunes us to that.

"THE CHANGING NAMES REFLECT THE NARRATOR'S CHANGING SITUATIONS, HER UNCERTAINTY ABOUT WHO SHE IS."

The first time Bailey Jr. uses the name "My," he does so while trying to reassure his sister about going to St. Louis with their father. "My, it's Mother Dear. You know you want to see Mother Dear. Don't cry." It could be the interjection "my," but we do realize that he's calling her by an affectionate nickname. Several pages later, Angelou explains the nickname. When she was a baby, Bailey, only a year older, referred to her as "mya sister." Later, he "elaborated" the name to Maya, which he then occasionally shortens to My. This particular derivation makes sense, but there's no explanation for some of the other name switches in the book—to Ritie, back to Marguerite, and so on. This naming confusion mirrors Angelou's confusion about her identity, her different identities in different cities that symbolize the sense of dislocation she felt throughout her childhood.

"RITIE IS THE NAME MOST CLOSELY ASSOCIATED WITH MR. FREEMAN'S ABUSE."

Angelou's Uncle Tommy, one of her mother's famously belligerent brothers, is the one who first calls her Ritie. He advises her not to worry about not being pretty, that it's better to have "a good mind than a cute behind." Everyone around Marguerite uses the new name matter-of-factly. It's fitting in the sense that Angelou felt "St. Louis was a foreign country," a place where none of the values Annie Henderson instilled in her in Stamps hold sway. That sense of dislocation comes across most strongly in Chapter 12, when Mr. Freeman uses the name in a series of ever more menacing commands: "Ritie, go get some milk for the house. . . . Ritie. Ritie, come here." Then, "I didn't mean to hurt you, Ritie. I didn't mean it." Having been molested and raped as Ritie, Angelou can do nothing but go back to being Marguerite, back to Stamps.

"THE NAME MARY IS AN IMPORTANT ONE, SINCE IT FIGURES IN ONE OF THE BOOK'S MOST TELLING EPISODES."

In Stamps, Marguerite briefly works for a white woman named Viola Cullinan, a native Virginian who is inhumanly demanding about how things must be done in her house. Marguerite devotes an uncharacteristic amount of space to her description of working for Mrs. Cullinan, especially the woman's refusal to call Marguerite by her proper name. Mrs. Cullinan tells some houseguests that her servant's name is Margaret, but since that's too long a name, everyone should call her Mary instead. At the time, Marguerite is in her silent period, refusing to talk to anyone except Bailey. She rebels against the name by neglecting her duties, arriving late and leaving early, and finally deliberately breaking several of Mrs. Cullinan's most beloved pieces of china. When a friend asks if "Mary" was responsible for the broken dishes, an enraged Mrs. Cullinan replies, "Her name's Margaret, goddamn it, her name's Margaret." Angelou explains her behavior from an adult perspective: "Every person I knew had a hellish horror of being 'called out of his name.' It was a dangerous practice to call a Negro anything that could be loosely construed as insulting because of the centuries of their having been called niggers, jigs, dinges, blackbirds, crows, boots and spooks." This explanation is a powerful passage. It accentuates the fact that the events that happen to Marguerite, Ritie, and Maya are, in a way, happening to different people.

○ ○ ○

What role does the town of Stamps play in Angelou's life? At first it seems like a poor, backward place, but is that accurate?

"STAMPS IS MUCH MORE THAN THAT—IT'S AN INSPIRATIONAL, INSTRUCTIONAL, AND RESTORATIVE PLACE."

It's a sophisticated Maya Angelou who makes many of the observations about Stamps, especially about its racial prejudice and crushing poverty. But the impressionable Marguerite tells about "those tender mornings" when the harsh reality of Stamps is "softened by nature's blessing of grogginess, forgetfulness, and the soft lamplight." Marguerite's description of the Store in morning time, "like an unopened present from a stranger," is one of the most vivid passages in the book. You can see the soft light and smell the scent of sardines, pickles, tobacco, and flour. Although Stamps is a poor, backward, racist place, it's a home for her, a place where Marguerite, at least, feels a kind of comfort and safety.

"STAMPS IS CLOSELY ASSOCIATED WITH MOMMA, WHO HAS AN IMMENSE MORAL AND SPIRITUAL ROLE IN THE CHILDREN'S LIVES."

Momma is the pillar both of the community as a whole and of her family. One of the most important episodes in the book is the unsuccessful attempt by several "powhitetrash" girls to humiliate her. Momma's dignity and integrity during this horrifying incident makes a lasting impact on the young Angelou. "Her face was a brown moon that shone on me," Marguerite remembers. "Whatever the contest had been out front, I knew Momma had won." Lessons like this one influence both Marguerte and Bailey, teaching them the values of dignity, faith, and perseverance in the face of a society that is often hostile.

"COMING BACK TO STAMPS FROM ST. LOUIS AFTER THE RAPE IS A KIND OF HEALING, A RETURN TO A PROTECTIVE WOMB."

Returning to her identity as Marguerite from the unpleasant associations of Ritie, Angelou welcomes the return to Stamps. Physically, the town is a barren place with obscure roads and lonely houses, but its resigned inhabitants are possessed of "a contentment based on the belief that nothing more was coming to them, although a great deal more was due." In Stamps, Marguerite learns to not only accept life's inequities, but to be satisfied with them. After Marguerite's return, it's the aristocratic Mrs. Bertha Flowers who gently coaxes her out of her lengthy silence. Mrs. Flowers calls Marguerite by her name: "My name was beautiful when she said it." The name tells us much about Angelou's condition at the time she's being named.

○　○　○

Is Ritie being realistic when she believes she can never forgive herself for telling the lie that indirectly leads to Freeman's death?

"THE LIE IS NECESSARY BECAUSE THE TRUTH WOULD BE MISLEADING."

Freeman's lawyer asks Ritie if Freeman ever touched her before he raped her. As young as she is, and as shattered by the experience as she is, she knows that if she tells the truth that he masturbated while in bed with her, the community will view her as responsible for the rape. Society will think she provoked further advances by assenting to the first abuse. Her family will be disappointed in and even alienated from her. The awful paradox is that the truth will set Freeman free and make a prisoner of Ritie for the rest of her life. She *has* to lie—probably every reader finally believes that—but she may also *have* to clear her conscience of the lie in the extreme way she chooses, by not speaking.

"IT'S FREEMAN WHOSE BEHAVIOR FORCES THE LIE, WHICH ONCE AGAIN MAKES RITIE HIS VICTIM."

After the rape, Ritie is too stunned to be angry with Freeman. It's shocking for us to read her admission that she almost enjoys the feeling of being cool and clean after he washes her in the bathtub. She does everything Freeman orders her to do because of her fear that he'll follow through on his threat to kill Bailey if she tells on him. Only in court, when Ritie realizes that she has to lie if her spirit is to survive, does she express her hatred for Freeman. She hates him not only for the rape, but also "for making me lie." The words Angelou gives Ritie at this point are tragic in their childishness and their inadequacy: "Old mean, nasty thing. Old, black, nasty thing."

"RITIE'S VICTIMHOOD CONTINUES EVEN AFTER THE FORCED LIE, WHEN FREEMAN IS ASSAULTED AND KILLED."

After the trial, Ritie and Bailey play Monopoly, an almost unbearably poignant reminder that she's still a child. A policeman arrives with the news that Freeman is dead, but of course Ritie assumes at first that the officer is there to arrest her for perjury. When she hears the news, she again feels responsible. She feels full of evil, certain that it will flow out of her and corrupt the world if she opens her mouth and lets it free. It's this sense of shock and guilt that prompts her momentous decision not to speak for so long afterward.

Marguerite's long period of silence is a powerful episode, but Angelou writes little about it. Is this disappointing or appropriate?

"SHE PROBABLY TELLS EVERYTHING SHE CAN TELL. HER SILENCE ABOUT HER SILENCE IS SOMEHOW FITTING."

The term hadn't been invented yet, but Angelou was suffering from post-traumatic stress disorder. It's striking that she *doesn't* say, "I stopped talking," which would imply a conscious, willful effort on her part. Instead she says, "I had to stop talking," meaning that her silence was really beyond her control and was brought about by circumstances. By lying about Freeman's first advances toward her, she feels she has ensured his conviction and thereby contributed to the retaliatory murder—a kind of lynching (although the culprits are probably Vivian's brothers, Ritie's uncles). Ritie, having accomplished so much (willfully or not) by talking, now can do nothing but *not* talk, to "achieve perfect personal silence."

"WE STILL LEARN A LOT ABOUT THIS PERIOD IN MARGUERITE'S LIFE. DURING HER SILENCE, SHE ISN'T CUT OFF FROM THE WORLD."

Marguerite's silence isn't completely isolating. She continues to be part of the world, a world that's full of sound. She says that after deciding that she won't talk, she begins listening to everything. The trip to St. Louis has made celebrities of Marguerite and Bailey, and people come from all over Stamps to hear about their adventures. Bailey can't resist telling stories and embellishing them, describing to his naïve audiences skyscrapers so high their tops are lost in the clouds, snow so deep it buries people right outside their doors for entire winters, cotton so high it has to be picked on ladders. Bailey talks so much, and with such artistry, that people start comparing him to his silver-tongued father. Marguerite is right there, recording his words and weaving them into her narrative. We learn as much from her accounts of listening as we do from her accounts as a participant in conversation.

"WE LEARN A GREAT DEAL ABOUT MARGUERITE IN HER MEETING WITH MRS. FLOWERS, WHO UNDERSTANDS HER SILENCE."

Friends and neighbors in Stamps view Marguerite's silence as a form of mourning for the big city of St. Louis, and as a manifestation of what Angelou calls "tender-heartedness," an oversensitivity that produces delicate health and chronic mild illness. And they mistake their incorrect diagnosis for an understanding of what's going on with Marguerite. The aristocratic Mrs. Flowers sees beyond the symptoms of Marguerite's silence to the profound root cause. Interestingly, the silent Marguerite is first drawn to Mrs. Flowers because of Mrs. Flowers's relationship with Momma—a woman who, in Marguerite's view, won't talk correctly. Embarrassed by her grandmother's diction and grammar, Marguerite is struck that the educated Mrs. Flowers treats her grandmother as an equal.

The scene that culminates with Marguerite's finally speaking again is almost like a seduction. Momma embarrasses Marguerite by ordering her to take her dress off in front of Mrs. Flowers in order to show the stitching. On the way to her house, Mrs. Flowers doesn't mention the disrobing, and she urges Marguerite to walk beside her rather than respectfully walk a few steps behind. Mrs. Flowers then carefully presents a case for the value of speech, admitting from the outset that no one can *force* Marguerite to talk. Mrs. Flowers reads to the girl from Dickens's *A Tale of Two Cities*. Marguerite realizes that Mrs. Flowers expects a response. "I had to speak," she says, just as earlier she has said, "I had to stop talking." It isn't an answer to the question she has been asked, but it's both the least and the most she could do. This remarkable awakening to the power of speech is a powerful depiction both of the end of Marguerite's silence and the graceful power of the lovely Mrs. Flowers.

What are we to make of Vivian Baxter, Angelou's mother?

"VIVIAN IS THE STAR OF HER OWN LIFE, BUT BY NO MEANS THE STAR OF HER DAUGHTER'S LIFE."

Angelou's first descriptions of her mother are fascinating—a hurricane, a rainbow, too beautiful for motherhood. But interestingly, having described her mother, Angelou turns her back on her. Ritie's first impressions of St. Louis are of Grandmother Baxter, of the gold-rush atmosphere of the city, of ham sandwiches and peanuts mixed with jelly beans, of the students at Toussaint L'Ouverture Grammar School. Ritie and Bailey seldom see their mother unless they go to Louie's tavern, where they are known as "Bibbie's little darlings," fed shrimp and sodas while their mother dances alone in front of them "like a pretty kite." But the lovely Vivian has a violent streak. She nearly kills a man with a billy club and silently threatens her children that their punishment for disobedience would be a return to Arkansas. Ritie conveys her own sadness at her mother's emotional distance by painting a remarkably sensitive portrait of Mr. Freeman, big and flabby and marked by "the sluggish inferiority of old men married to young women." Though Mr. Freeman is ultimately a despicable character, Angelou nonetheless understands her mother's remoteness as a cause of his loneliness and frustration.

"IT'S HARD TO FORGET THAT VIVIAN INDIRECTLY SETS THE STAGE FOR THE RAPE, BRINGING RITIE INTO BED WITH HER AND MR. FREEMAN."

St. Louis is a foreign land to Ritie and Bailey. They outshine their peers in school, but they're so unhappy that Bailey often stutters and Ritie has nightmares. Bibbie's solution to the nightmares, with its awful outcome, contradicts Angelou's assessment that her mother "was competent in providing for us." Though trained as a nurse, Bibbie doesn't have anything one could call a real job, allowing herself to be kept by Mr. Freeman, earning money on the side by dealing poker games in gambling halls. We're left with the feeling that Bibbie is not only too beautiful for motherhood, but too irresponsible.

"BIBBIE'S EVENTUAL RESPONSE TO THE RAPE IS TO SEND RITIE AWAY AGAIN—HARDLY A LOVING GESTURE."

Two key paragraphs in Chapter 13 describe Ritie's getting a clean bill of health from a visiting nurse and a doctor during her recuperation from the rape. They consider her "healed," implying that she should instantly become a normal child again. When Ritie is unable to suddenly re-assume her old self, her family members label her "impudent" and sullen. At first, she is punished. Then come the "thrashings," administered by any family member who happens to take offense at her behavior.

In the next paragraph, without explanation or elaboration, we see the children on their way back to Stamps, with Ritie trying to console Bailey, who is pressed against the window striving for a glimpse of his "Mother Dear." In retrospect, Angelou guesses that either Sister Henderson sent for them or the St. Louis family tired of them. It's remarkable that she chooses not to speculate about her mother's role in the decision. If Bibbie is too beautiful for motherhood, she's certainly too beautiful to provide the kind of sympathy and empathy that a raped child would require. Ritie says she was only concerned that Bailey was unhappy and "had no more thought of our destination than if I had simply been heading for the toilet." The image is striking. It conveys Ritie's self-loathing, which her mother and her mother's family do nothing to ease.

○　○　○

How do we feel on learning that the children are to rejoin Vivian in California?

"NOT OPTIMISTIC. VIVIAN TAKES THEM BACK ONLY BECAUSE MOMMA'S CONCERNED THAT BAILEY IS MISERABLE."

Vivian doesn't exactly pine away for the children after they leave St. Louis or pester Momma to send them back to California. But Bailey never adjusts after leaving his mother in St. Louis and going back to

Stamps. At one point he convinces himself that the white movie actress Kay Francis is actually Vivian. The only reason he and Marguerite are sent back to California is because Momma considers it necessary after Bailey's scare regarding the black man's corpse. There's no mention of how Vivian feels about becoming a mother again. Tragically, Marguerite feels no thrill of anticipation at seeing her mother, only her old guilt about Mr. Freeman: "I was as unprepared to meet my mother as a sinner is reluctant to meet his Maker."

"WE STILL FEEL SOME HOPE WHEN RITIE FINALLY SEES HER MOTHER."

Vivian has charisma, there's no doubt about that. She sweeps Ritie off her feet, a smaller woman than Ritie remembers, but more glorious than ever in her suede suit and matching shoes, her feathered hat, her lipstick, and her gloved hands. She expertly arranges for the children's luggage to be cared for, she impresses the children with her apartment and its exotic convertible sofa. Urbane and sophisticated, she puts her daughter into a kind of trance that suppresses all her anxieties. We wonder if her sheer charm and joy in living will be enough to make up for her hands-off attitude toward the children.

"EVEN IF WE HAVE INITIAL HOPE, VIVIAN DISAPPOINTS US AGAIN. SHE ABANDONS NOT ONLY HER CHILDREN BUT MOMMA AS WELL."

Ritie, Bailey, and Momma Henderson live in Los Angeles for six months while Vivian makes arrangements for the children to live with her in San Francisco. We start to wonder what is taking so long. Momma and the children's isolation in a strange city isn't helped by the occasional appearances of Bailey Sr., carrying shopping bags of fruit, blessing them with his presence "like a Sun God," then returning to his girlfriend (or girlfriends). Angelou comments less on the behavior of her parents than on the "remarkable adjustment" to life in California her grandmother makes. Momma has never been exposed to such a big city or such a diverse population—whites, Mexicans, African Americans who aren't her intimate friends, as in Stamps, but ordinary urban strangers next door.

Learning that Momma is going back to Stamps, Ritie makes the striking comment that she'd be willing to accompany Momma even if her beloved brother were to remain behind.

The woman Ritie and Bailey call Momma goes back to her home in Arkansas, leaving them in the care of the woman they call Mother. We see Vivian as a pinochle and poker dealer whose idea of a good time includes waking her children at 2:30 in the morning for hot chocolate and brown biscuits. Angelou uses positive adjectives and verbs to describe Vivian, but the anecdotes she tells often contradict the words she employs. Contradiction is Vivian's middle name: she's jolly but merciless, angry but fair, impartial but not indulgent. Before the children arrive from Arkansas, we learn that Vivian had previously beaten a man with a billy club and shot another man with a revolver. The man didn't die and retaliated by striking Vivian, bruising her face. In recounting the story, Angelou admires Vivian's fairness in warning the man she was going to fire the gun, and, in turn, admires the man's ability to inflict two black eyes on Vivian. "Admirable qualities," the adult Angelou comments, but she doesn't tell us what Ritie thought of the incident. Can anyone who has been raped think of violent behavior as an admirable quality?

○ ○ ○

What role does the move to San Francisco play in Ritie's life?

"AT THE OUTSET, WE'RE APPREHENSIVE BECAUSE WE KNOW VIVIAN'S FAMILY IS THERE."

San Francisco is "St. Louis revisited," Angelou writes. Uncles Tommy and Billy—the ones we suspect of the revenge murder of Mr. Freeman—are there, as is their mother, the chain-smoking Grandma Baxter. Learning that Ritie has to share a bed with an adult again makes us cringe, even though this time her bedmate is her grandmother, whose nicotine addiction is so strong that she frequently wakes coughing violently in the night, finally lighting up cigarettes to soothe her throat. It hardly seems like an ideal family environment. Even though there's poverty in Stamps, we feel that Momma is a strong pillar for Marguerite and Bailey. Now that pillar is gone—we've seen what happened in St. Louis, and we worry history will repeat itself.

"AS RITIE GRADUALLY GETS TO KNOW THE CITY, WE FEEL THE ANXIETY EASE—ODDLY ENOUGH, ON THE BRINK OF WORLD WAR II."

Angelou's descriptions of San Francisco in the early months of the war are some of the most evocative in the book. She conveys the transformation of the Fillmore District from a Japanese enclave to a "Harlem West" by describing how the odors of Japanese cooking give way to those of African-American cuisine. Her observations about the city, which "acted in wartime like an intelligent woman under siege," are not Ritie's at all, but those of a mature, experienced observer recollecting events from the distance of decades. That observer remarks that Ritie, for the first time, felt part of a *place*, a place that intoxicates even as it infuriates with its silent racism and mistrust of people with yellow or black skin. Ritie is less a girl in San Francisco and more an "intelligent woman" herself.

"RITIE ALSO ACQUIRES A FATHER IN SAN FRANCISCO, QUITE UNEXPECTEDLY."

In one stark paragraph, Ritie tells us Vivian is getting married, then introduces us to her new stepfather, Daddy Clidell. Though Ritie says that he "turned out to be the first father I would know," we're justifiably nervous about the future of these relationships—mother and husband, stepfather and stepdaughter, daughter and mother. We especially worry because, after introducing Daddy Clidell, Ritie then drops him out of the book for nearly a dozen pages. She admits that she expected Clidell, an uneducated owner of apartment buildings and pool halls, to be just one more soulless conquest of Vivian's. But Clidell surpasses Ritie's expectations by behaving with simplicity and honesty, even while teaching Ritie and Bailey how to play poker, blackjack, and other card games, and introducing them to his colorful friends, every one of them a con artist. Oddly, we get the sense of a new, unconventional type of family surrounding Ritie, and we worry less about her future than we do when she first arrives in San Francisco.

What's the nature of Marguerite's relationship with Bailey Sr. during her stay in California?

"IT'S HEARTBREAKING TO SEE MARGUERITE'S HOPE WHEN WE KNOW FROM THE START THE TRIP TO MEXICO WILL BE A DISASTER."

Marguerite's visit to Los Angeles and Mexico with Bailey Sr. and Dolores has the quality of a fantasy. Marguerite professes a good deal of contempt for Dolores, but it's really her father who is the object of her venom. Late in the book, we learn for the first time of Bailey Sr.'s service in the army during World War I, his former job as a doorman at the "exclusive" Breakers' Hotel, his current job "in the kitchen" of a naval hospital in Los Angeles, which he claims is a position as a "medical dietician for the United States Navy." We also learn that Bailey Sr. had promised to marry Dolores but was apparently married to yet another woman, whom we never meet, named Alberta.

Angelou's description of her happiness at the outset of her "foreign adventure" with her father is unconvincing. And her reactions to her first views of Mexico and Mexicans convey a desperate effort to appear to be having a good time. Her comment that half the people look like young, handsome movie stars, the other half like aging character actors sounds like the observation of an unthoughtful American tourist abroad. All this contributes to a feeling of unease. There's a sense of tremendous discon-nection in this section of the book, of us watching Angelou watching Marguerite watching herself.

"THESE FEELINGS OF ANXIETY ARE JUSTIFIED, GIVEN BAILEY'S BEHAVIOR IN THE CANTINA."

Bailey Sr. transforms in Marguerite's eyes, from a lonely, inept man whose way of speaking continually embarrasses her to a relaxed, handsome, black American, speaking fluent Spanish, and spending money freely. But this change in her opinion of him is pathetic and frightening to watch. We know that Bailey Sr. is about to go off with a Mexican woman, abandoning his daughter yet again, this time among strangers in a strange land. When he finally returns, drunk, Marguerite once again is stuck coping with an irresponsible adult. She has no choice but to drive a car for the first time in her life, fifty miles down a dark, dangerous mountain road. Her pride in her accomplishment does little to assuage our anxiety on her behalf. We want to think that the episode might at least be another growth experience for Marguerite, but Angelou denies us this comfort by undercutting virtually every one of Marguerite's optimistic sentiments almost immediately, somtimes even in the next sentence.

○　○　○

How do the adventures with Bootsie and his gang transform Marguerite?

"IN A SENSE, MARGUERITE'S BEEN PREPARING FOR THIS EXPERIENCE EVER SINCE SHE LEARNED TO READ."

The penny arcades tempt Marguerite, but she goes to the library, to change her bandages and to read science fiction. It's important to remember that after her rape she went to the library too. The world of literature is her safe haven. After all, she's admitted that her first white love was Shakespeare. She certainly succeeds in stimulating her imagination in a way that anesthetizes her from pain and loneliness. She thinks of the abandoned car she sleeps in as an island and the junkyard in which it stands as a sea separating her from the dangerous mainland.

"MARGUERITE'S INVOLVEMENT WITH A MULTIRACIAL, MULTIETHNIC GROUP OF CHILDREN HELPS HER FIND HER SENSE OF SELF."

At first, Marguerite thinks that the children, who tower over her makeshift bed, are adults—maybe even the giant Brobdingnagians from Jonathan Swift's *Gulliver's Travels*. But reading her story about the tall boy "who said he was Bootsie," we may be reminded more of J.M. Barrie's *Peter Pan*. We never learn Bootsie's story, just as we never learn Peter's. Bootsie is the ringleader and rule-maker: no boy-girl sleeping pairs, no stealing, no slacking off because everyone in the gang has to work. Marguerite tells the group she is called Maya—an interesting declaration of self. She asserts herself even more in a jitterbug contest that all the kids enter to increase the group's odds of winning. She and her partner, Juan, come in second even though their dance technique resembles wrestling or hand-to-hand combat. Altogether, Maya finds unconditional acceptance for her new self during this time on her own, an important episode in her life that gives her strength that she draws on later.

"ANGELOU PACKS A MONTH INTO TWO PAGES, SO WE HAVE TO TAKE HER WORD FOR IT THAT THE GANG EXPERIENCE TRANSFORMS HER."

The paragraph summing up her experience with Bootsie's gang is full of self-awareness and self-confidence. For the first time, she *is* Maya. Maya's thinking has changed unrecognizably. Her old insecurity is gone. Having gone beyond the pale, she feels paradoxically part of "the brotherhood of man." The gang's uncritical acceptance instills in her a lifelong tolerance. But despite this transformation, we remain apprehensive because the next thing Maya does is go home to her mother, never telling Vivian about Mexico, the stabbing, or her life on the street. Maya calls Dolores a liar for having called Vivian a whore, but we also feel the significance of Maya's white lie, her glossing over her trying experience in Southern California. We know the price Maya has paid in the past by keeping things to herself.

Marguerite changes obviously and drastically throughout the book. What changes does Bailey undergo?

"BAILEY'S THE POLAR OPPOSITE OF HIS SISTER FROM THE START, A BORN EXTROVERT AND A COMPASSIONATE BROTHER."

In Stamps, Bailey stops for a few minutes with everyone the children meet on their walks through the black part of town. In St. Louis, he plays quizmaster, asking crowds of boys in the playground who Napoleon was and how many feet there are in a mile. Ritie says that she and Bailey started to grow apart, and that she spent her Saturdays in the library while he went out. But the only evidence we have of that is her word, and it may be that she grows more introverted while he stays the same. Bailey's tenderness when Ritie is raped displays the compassion and closeness we've seen all along. And it's Bailey who tells Grandmother Baxter about the rape, ignoring Freeman's threat. Bailey sneaks into the hospital during Ritie's recuperation and reads to her for hours. We see this compassion most strongly during the aftermath of the rape, but it's there in Bailey all along.

"BAILEY'S ENCOUNTER WITH HIS MOTHER MAKES HIM GROW IMMENSELY. THEN HIS LOSS OF HER CAUSES A HEARTBREAKING CHANGE IN HIM."

Ritie is genuinely upset at Bailey's misery. She might be even more upset to see him becoming like his father, telling tall tales about life in St. Louis, discovering a gift for sarcasm and double entendre, hopping a freight train and trying to get to California to see his mother, playing "Momma and Poppa" with girls, stealing from the Store for Joyce. Marguerite's assessment of Joyce is striking: Bailey thinks of Joyce as a mother who lets him get as close as he wants, as a sister who isn't moody and depressed. Bailey's exposure to his mother and then separation from her makes him aware of the void that's been in his life all along, and it forces him to grow up suddenly, much as the trauma of the rape causes Marguerite to grow up too fast.

"THE BLACK MAN'S CORPSE IS A SHOCKING EXPOSURE TO RACISM THAT FOREVER COSTS BAILEY HIS INNOCENCE."

Bailey's sight of the corpse of a black man and the white man's racist response causes the most jarring change we ever see in the boy. Momma is so concerned about Bailey that she personally takes the children to California, even though it means making special arrangements for someone to mind the store and to care for the crippled Uncle Willie. We wonder if Momma is concerned about the effects of the move on Marguerite, who, after all, was sexually assaulted the last time she lived in a big city with her mother. It seems that Momma feels that young black men are more imperiled than young black women. Angelou describes "the enigma that young Southern Black boys start to unravel, start to *try* to unravel, from seven years old to death. The humorless puzzle of inequality and hate." Bailey's experience with the corpse finally awakens him to the reality of racism and the odds stacked against him. He's never the same after this awakening.

○   ○   ○

We see a great deal of Momma in the book, especially in the first half. But does that mean we really know her well?

"YES, WE KNOW HER VERY WELL. MOMMA'S LIKE AN ARCHETYPE FROM FICTION—THE UNEDUCATED BUT WISE, PIOUS WOMAN WHO IS A PILLAR OF HER FAMILY AND COMMUNITY."

Momma is a remarkably successful businesswoman, thanks in part to her "miraculous ability to be in two places at the same time." She's physically imposing, formerly pretty, still good-looking. She's soft-spoken but allows herself every week to be coaxed to sing in a "huge, almost rough" voice. She's a realist when it comes to dealing with white people, preferring not to talk to them at all but knowing she can't afford to be insolent when she does. When Bailey Sr. takes the children to St. Louis, she keeps her opinion about the move to herself. She only hopes that people will feel she raised the children properly. She's an archetype of the grandmother who has done her best to shape her grandchildren with her values. She realizes that she's done all she can and that the children must eventually grow up and go off on their own.

Momma's departure from California is also her departure from Angelou's memoir. Once again we feel a sense of dread on learning that the children are confronting yet another change. Marguerite says, "She had done her job. . . . We had our own parents at last." But she immediately undercuts that positive declaration, saying, "At least we were in the same state." Momma's departure signals the end of childhood for Marguerite and Bailey. They are going to live with their mother, but they have lost their Momma, their true mother figure.

"NO, MOMMA CAN'T BE REDUCED TO A CHARACTER TYPE. SHE'S DIFFICULT TO KNOW. EVEN MARGUERITE DOESN'T KNOW HER WELL."

In the opening paragraph of the chapter about the children's journey to California, Angelou says, "Knowing Momma, I knew that I never knew Momma." We suddenly realize that we don't know how Momma has felt about many things—the move to St. Louis, the rape, the children's return, and now their departure. Momma is a quiet enigma. Angelou provides a complicated explanation of Momma's personality, the "African-bush secretiveness and suspiciousness . . . compounded by slavery and confirmed by centuries of promises made and promises broken." This generalization comes from the adult Angelou stiltedly justifying Momma's refusal to talk to her grandchildren about emotions, any emotions. For all we know about Momma's outward actions, we never know much about her inner life—and we sense that Angelou tries to gloss over her own lack of knowledge about Momma as well.

○ ○ ○

Caged Bird relates many painful racist experiences. Do these elicit anger or racial pride? Or both?

"THERE'S A LOT OF ANGER IN THE BOOK, BUT ALSO AN OVERWHELMING SENSE OF PRIDE IN BEING BLACK."

The chapter about the heavyweight fight is striking for its power and brevity. It's only four pages long, but it's written in vivid, descriptive language. It comes across like a newspaper account of the fight itself—only it's an account of the crowd's *reaction* to the fight on the radio. When things go badly for Louis, "my race groaned," Angelou writes. When Louis fights back and finally knocks Primo Carnera out, "[p]eople drank Coca-Colas like ambrosia and ate candy bars like Christmas." But at the end of the chapter, there's anxiety about walking home on dark country roads—"on a night when Joe Louis had proved that we were the strongest people in the world."

"THE ANGER OFTEN DOES BURST FORTH, AS WE SEE IN THE GRADUATION SCENE."

Marguerite makes this realization during her graduation from Lafayette County Training School, another proud moment that's tinged with racism. Marguerite's excitement on graduation day is charming and moving, especially since she realizes that her eighth-grade education puts her on par with many of the African-American teachers in Arkansas. She likes her dress, she even likes her unruly hair. But a white graduation speaker, identified only as "Mr. Edward Donleavy. . . from Texarkana," insults all the graduates by talking only about the athletic accomplishments of other black graduates before them. Yes, Marguerite says, Louis and Jesse Owens were great heroes to the black people, but not their only heroes.

"EVEN THOUGH THE BOOK IS ANGRY, THE ANGER IS JUSTIFIED, AND THE SENSE OF PRIDE DEFINITELY WINS OUT IN THE END."

The graduation ends with a note of pride rather than the anger that characterizes the whole book. The class saves the day by leading the singing of "Lift Ev'ry Voice and Sing." Afterward, Marguerite has three brief thoughts: "We were on top again. As always, again. We survived." The voice of the adult Angelou rises to the tone of an ode as she praises black poets, preachers, musicians, blues singers, and others for the contributions they've made to the survival of the black race. Angelou often expresses contempt for white people, but the behavior of the whites she describes is often contemptible. Her anger is never irrational, and she more often praises her own people rather than deride whites.

○ ○ ○

Is the overall tone of the memoir optimistic or pessimistic?

"IT'S VERY OPTIMISTIC—MAYA IS A SURVIVOR, SO WE FEEL A SENSE OF TRIUMPH OVER TREMENDOUS ODDS."

After all she's been through, there's little doubt that Maya will continue to prevail over the obstacles she finds in her path. If Vivian is there to help her, all the better, but Maya has crafted her responses to adversity on her own. She's grown from a practically motherless child to the mother of a child, all the while relying on her own strength and independence. If we feel optimistic about her future, it isn't because Vivian is there to instill confidence; it is because Maya has won us over with her determination.

"NOT NECESSARILY—KNOWING MAYA IS UNDER VIVIAN'S CARE MAKES US MORE NERVOUS THAN HOPEFUL."

The big question about Vivian, always in the back of our minds, is "where will she go next?" It wouldn't be much of a surprise if we learned that Vivian plans to send Maya and her new baby back to Arkansas, to Momma Henderson's care. Vivian's advice about seeing and doing the right thing is almost laughable when we think about her own unpredictable and irresponsible behavior. The best we can feel about Maya is relief that her father isn't around. Daddy Clidell is finally an adult man in her life with some maturity and stability. On the whole, we're left with a lot of uncertainty at the end.

"IT'S A MOOT POINT BECAUSE WE HAVE THE BENEFIT OF 20/20 HINDSIGHT."

Most of us who pick up the memoir have at least a vague awareness of Maya Angelou's life—that she's one of America's best-known writers, women, and African Americans. So knowing that she ultimately finds fame and success, we read her memoir as a traditional coming of age story. We know with confidence that the future that awaits Marguerite at the end of the book is one that she'll safely and successfully traverse, no matter how difficult the passage. I Know Why the Caged Bird Sings is more a story of the triumph of perseverance in a young person. The whole issue of optimism vs. pessimism doesn't really apply—we can get more from the book just by looking at it as a chronicle rather than an outlook for the future.

A Golden Voice

Angelou has an unequaled place in
American culture—a giant in letters,
poetry, civil rights, feminism, and oratory.

○　○　○

"YOU'RE GOING TO BE FAMOUS," Billie Holiday once told Maya
Angelou, "but it won't be for singing." The famous blues singer rendered
that opinion of the would-be calypso singer Angelou during an encounter
in Los Angeles in 1958. At the time, Angelou had worked as a streetcar
conductor and a brothel madam, among other jobs, but had never published a word, though she had been an avid reader since early childhood.
(Shakespeare, Angelou writes in *I Know Why the Caged Bird Sings*, "was
my first white love.") Perhaps, in their unlikely five-day visit (recounted in
First Encounters, by Edward and Nancy Sorel), Holiday heard Angelou
telling anecdotes of her upbringing in a tiny Arkansas town during the
Depression, in Prohibition-era St. Louis, and in World War II San Francisco and knew she had an important story to tell—one that would find
an audience that continually replenished itself.

Angelou's early life is familiar to readers of *I Know Why the Caged
Bird Sings*. She was born Marguerite Johnson in St. Louis on April 4,
1928, to Bailey Johnson, a doorman and dietician, and Vivian Baxter
Johnson, a nurse and real-estate agent. When the Great Depression took
hold of the country, the Johnsons moved to Los Angeles in search of better opportunities. They found few, however, so Bailey and Vivian sent
Marguerite and her older brother, Bailey Jr., to Stamps, Arkansas, to the
care of their paternal grandmother, Annie Henderson. Marguerite and
Bailey moved three more times before they were teenagers: to St. Louis,

A penny for her thoughts

In 2002, Hallmark Cards, Inc., hired Angelou to write the text for a new line of greeting cards, pillows, sachets, and collectibles. Angelou dismissed critics who accused her of selling out, telling the *New York Times,* "If I'm the people's poet, then my work should be in the people's hands. There are many people who will never buy a book, but who would buy a card."

where Vivian's boyfriend raped Marguerite; back to Stamps; then to San Francisco. While still in high school, Marguerite worked as a streetcar conductor, the first African American to be hired as a conductor in San Francisco. She gave birth to a son, Guy, in 1945—the point at which the narrative of *I Know Why the Caged Bird Sings* ends.

Angelou's first artistic endeavors were as a singer and dancer. She had a part in a U.S. State Department-sponsored production of *Porgy and Bess* that visited twenty-two nations during 1954 and 1955. She then appeared in two off-Broadway plays, *Calypso Heatwave* (1957) and Jean Genet's *The Blacks* (1960). Angelou's collaboration with Godfrey Cambridge, *Cabaret for Freedom*, ran off-Broadway in 1960. Throughout the following decade, Angelou traveled and lived in Africa, working as a magazine editor in Cairo and a university lecturer and administrator in Accra, Ghana.

Angelou was also involved in the civil rights movement, becoming the Northern Coordinator for Dr. Martin Luther King Jr.'s Southern Christian Leadership Conference. As an artist she continued to focus on the stage. She appeared in a production of *Medea* in Los Angeles in 1966 and debuted on Broadway in 1973 in the play *Look Away*, receiving a Tony nomination for her acting. (The award went to Julie Harris for *The Last of Mrs. Lincoln*.) By then, *I Know Why the Caged Bird Sings* had been published to critical and popular acclaim in 1969. From that point onward, Angelou's life is a litany of accomplishments in a range of genres and a study in ever-increasing celebrity.

Angelou gained recognition among a wider audience in 1977, when she appeared in the TV miniseries *Roots*, based on Alex Haley's 1976 book dramatizing his ancestors' forced migration from Africa to the American South. The third-largest audience in television history saw Angelou play Nyo Boto, the grandmother of Haley's ancestor Kunta Kinte. (The large cast also included Cicely Tyson, O.J. Simpson, and Louis Gossett, Jr.) Angelou received an Emmy nomination for her performance.

The second and third volumes of Angelou's memoir, *Gather Together in My Name* and *Singin' and Swingin' and Gettin' Merry Like Christmas* were published in 1974 and 1976, respectively. Her book of poetry *Just Give Me a Cool Drink of Water 'fore I Diiie* (1971) received a Pulitzer Prize nomination in 1972. Another collection of poems, *Oh Pray My Wings Are Gonna Fit Me Well* was published in 1975. In 1983, *Ladies' Home Journal* named Angelou one of the 100 most influential women in America, a well-deserved honor.

Angelou has amassed numerous awards and honorary degrees over the years. She was a member of President Ford's American Revolutionary Bicentennial Advisory Council and President Carter's National Commission on the Observance of International Women's Year. She wrote and delivered a poem, "On the Pulse of Morning," for President Clinton's first inauguration. Since 1981, Angelou has been Reynolds Professor of American Studies at Wake Forest University in Winston-Salem, North Carolina, a lifetime chair. She teaches a course on the philosophy of liberation. On top of it all, she speaks French, Spanish, Italian, Arabic, and West African Fanti.

Angelou's total body of work is vast: personal essays, children's books, poetry, plays, screenplays, teleplays, articles in periodicals from *Black Scholar* to *Mademoiselle*—not to mention acting appearances in television's *Touched by an Angel, Sesame Street,* and *Moesha* and in the films *How to Make an American Quilt* and *Down in the Delta*. Although she intends the sixth volume of her memoir, *A Song Flung Up to Heaven*

The nation's poet

"On the Pulse of Morning," which Maya Angelou delivered at President Bill Clinton's inauguration on January 20, 1993, was only the second poem to be read at a presidential swearing-in (the first being Robert Frost's "The Gift Outright" at President John F. Kennedy's inauguration in 1961). The town of Stamps, Arkansas, where Angelou spent a portion of her childhood, is only twenty-five miles from President Clinton's birthplace in the town of Hope, Arkansas.

(2002), to be her last, she continues to write poems and essays—even a cookbook. In an interview with the British newspaper *The Guardian*, Angelou described the following working routine: she rents a room in a motel, has all the decorations removed, and sits down with a thesaurus, a dictionary, a writing pad, and a bottle of sherry.

Of all her work, does Angelou have a favorite? It might be her PBS television documentary *Afro-American in the Arts*—for her co-producer was someone who will be familiar to readers of *I Know Why the Caged Bird Sings*: her son, Guy Johnson, whose birth ends the first volume of her memoir.

Red, White, Black and Blue

Angelou's early life plays out amid the slew of social and economic hardships America faced in the mid-twentieth century.

I KNOW WHY THE CAGED BIRD SINGS is above all a remarkable personal memoir, but it's also a portrait of a number of significant moments in American history—the Great Depression, racial segregation, the aftermath of Prohibition, and the home front during World War II.

THE GREAT DEPRESSION

Born in April 1928, Maya Angelou was just eighteen months old when the stock market crashed on Black Thursday, October 24, 1929. A number of different economic factors contributed to the catastrophic collapse. Goods were being overproduced. The wealth accumulated in the U.S. during the prosperous 1920s had been distributed unevenly, resulting in a lack of buying power among the general population. By the depth of the Great Depression, in 1932, sixteen million Americans were out of work— one out of every three available workers. The U.S. gross national product declined by nearly half.

The inauguration of President Franklin D. Roosevelt in March 1933 brought the beginnings of an economic recovery, as Roosevelt implemented a set of social and economic programs collectively called the New Deal. But the economy didn't truly recover until the early 1940s, when defense spending increased significantly during World War II. The war prompted businesses to rebound from the long slump and brought employment back to pre-crash levels.

Though the Depression was a difficult time for the entire nation, the worsening economy hit African Americans harder than any other group. Half of the black population lost their jobs—in many cases when they were fired to make jobs available to whites.

SEGREGATION

To be black in the United States from the Civil War era through the 1960s, especially in the South, was to live in a separate country. Yes, slavery had been abolished after the Southern states met defeat in the Civil War. But many factors—poll taxes, literacy tests, societal customs and attitudes—ensured that blacks continued to be denied an equal share in the social, legal, and political life of their communities. Separate bathrooms and drinking fountains, separate sections on buses and trains, separate hotels and motels, separate schools and colleges—even separate hospitals and jails—constituted the reality of life for black Americans until well into the twentieth century.

> To be black in the United States from the Civil War era through the 1960s, especially in the South, was to live in a separate country.

Particularly insidious was the Ku Klux Klan, an offshoot of a racist secret society that flourished during the period of Reconstruction just after the Civil War. Though the group's influence steadily declined over time, its assaults and lynchings of blacks continued well into the middle of the twentieth century. The KKK terrorized not only blacks, but also moderate whites who were sympathetic to black causes.

In the late 1800s and early 1900s, black voters had traditionally backed candidates from the Republican party—the party of the emancipator Abraham Lincoln. But the election of Franklin D. Roosevelt caused a sea change in the country's racial climate. Roosevelt had several black advisors and entertained African-American visitors at the White

House. Civil rights groups, foremost among them the National Association for the Advancement of Colored People (NAACP), had been formed and were gaining greater political influence.

But even though the tide seemed to be turning by FDR's administration, racism was still rampant. Roosevelt's New Deal economic programs, especially his housing and employment initiatives, were rife with discrimination. Plagued by political worries, Roosevelt didn't always support legislation that the NAACP proposed.

Then, World War II, much as it speeded economic recovery, hastened the progress of the civil rights cause as well. In 1941, labor leader A. Philip Randolph threatened to organize a march on Washington if discriminatory job practices in the military and the defense industry weren't changed. Recognizing the validity of Randolph's complaint, FDR issued an executive order stating that anyone, regardless of race, religion, or ethnicity, should have the full right to support the cause of defending the United States. After the war, further executive orders ended segregation in the armed forces. The legal tide continued to swing in favor of civil rights as courts gradually abolished or changed discriminatory laws.

In 1954, the Supreme Court ruled in the landmark case *Brown v. Board of Education of Topeka, Kansas* that segregation in public schools was illegal. Nonetheless, many African Americans were forced to continue to attend separate, inferior schools. Laws that forced blacks to use separate city buses, restaurants, hotels, public bathrooms, and water fountains remained on the books in many areas. Only in the 1960s, under the leadership of Martin Luther King Jr., Malcolm X, and Ralph Abernathy, did African Americans gain significant momentum in their campaigns against these discriminatory laws and in their drive for full, equal participation in American society.

PROHIBITION

From 1919 to 1933, it was illegal to produce, sell, import, or export alcoholic beverages in the United States. Even after the 21st Amendment repealed Prohibition, some states and cities retained the ban on alcohol. The St. Louis that Maya Angelou describes in the middle portion of her memoir was—and still is—famous for the production of beer and once had as many as fifty breweries in the city. The distilleries that produced bootleg liquor and the speakeasies where it was consumed were thriving businesses, and bribery and corruption of police and politicians was rampant.

Prohibition had been repealed by the time Angelou and her brother moved to St. Louis, but she writes about it as if it were still in effect—a reflection, probably, of the prevailing lawlessness that typified the period. Alcohol consumption declined about thirty percent during Prohibition and didn't return to pre-Prohibition levels until many years after repeal. However, given that illegal manufacture and consumption of alcohol was widespread during the period, it's arguable whether or not Prohibition was at all successful.

WORLD WAR II

Maya Angelou was just thirteen when the Japanese attacked Pearl Harbor and the U.S. entered World War II. For her, a major impact of the war was the virtual disappearance from the streets of San Francisco of the many Japanese and Chinese people who lived in the city. San Francisco's Fillmore District became known as "Harlem West" as large numbers of black people moved into the formerly Asian-American neighborhood.

During the war, San Francisco was part of a large area of the west coast from which everyone of Japanese ancestry was forced out. A Japanese submarine attack on a military supply depot in Oregon in June 1942 fueled a great deal of anti-Japanese sentiment in the U.S. The Japanese were not the only targets of war hysteria, though. A San Francisco newspaper reported in March 1942 that the Italian-born parents of baseball star Joe DiMaggio were suspected of being enemy agents.

The War Relocation Authority, under a policy known as internment, set up ten relocation centers for some 110,000 people of Japanese descent, most of them American citizens. The internment camps, located in remote areas of California, Arizona, Idaho, Wyoming, Colorado, Utah, and Arkansas, had guard towers, searchlights, and machine gun installations. Internees were divided into four categories: Issei, immigrants who had been born in Japan; Nisei, American-born and American-educated children of Issei; Sansei, American-born children of Nisei; and Kibei, those born in America but educated mostly in Japan. Lieutenant General

Maya's trades

Maya Angelou has worked as a streetcar conductor, a cook, a cocktail waitress, a dancer and bar girl, and the manager of a brothel. She bluffed her way into a gig as a calypso singer at the Purple Onion, a famous San Francisco nightclub where talent scouts invited her to join a touring company of *Porgy and Bess.*

John L. DeWitt, commander of the Fourth U.S. Army headquarters in San Francisco, oversaw much of the relocation effort. DeWitt rejected suggestions that the Issei and Nisei did not present any threat to U.S. security. "A Jap is a Jap," DeWitt said.

Some of those interned were permitted to leave the camps, provided they moved out of the Japanese-restricted area and had jobs. But most remained in the centers until December 1944, nine months before the end of the war in the Pacific. Some were relocated to new homes in the Midwest and Northeast. In 1988, President Ronald Reagan signed a law providing a payment of $20,000 in compensation to each surviving Japanese-American internee. The next year, President George Bush issued a formal apology to the internees from the U.S. government.

The African-American population of San Francisco and neighboring Oakland grew dramatically because of the war and the Japanese internment policy. Blacks from all over the South came to the Bay Area to work at naval shipyards. Many lived in Bayview-Hunters Point, next to a naval shipyard, others lived in the Fillmore District. Bayview-Hunters Point grew to become the city's largest African-American district. The Bayview Opera House, the Lorraine Hansberry Theatre, and the San Francisco African-American Museum are important centers of black culture in the city today. The Fillmore District attracted jazz and R&B musicians from around the U.S., and in the 1960s, along with the nearby Haight-Ashbury neighborhood, it was the center of the San Francisco sound of the Jefferson Airplane and other acid rock groups.

Breaking New Ground

I Know Why the Caged Bird Sings marked a new era in memoir, African-American writing, and women's writing.

○ ○ ○

I KNOW WHY THE CAGED BIRD SINGS was a remarkable success for any first book, but especially for a personal memoir by an unknown African-American woman who had hitherto been a streetcar conductor, a calypso singer, a madam, and an unwed mother.

The *New York Times* reviewed *I Know Why the Caged Bird Sings* on February 25, 1970, along with *Sugar Ray*, an as-told-to autobiography of boxer Sugar Ray Robinson. The *Times's* chief critic, Christopher Lehmann-Haupt, devoted the first half of his review to the Robinson book, which he read with "the nostalgic enjoyment of watching a forties movie on the Late Show." Clearly a fan of both boxing and Robinson, Lehmann-Haupt somewhat ruefully admitted that *Sugar Ray* (and probably Sugar Ray himself) was lacking in critical self-examination.

Turning to Angelou's book, Lehmann-Haupt called it "a carefully wrought, simultaneously touching and comic memoir of a black girl's slow and clumsy growth to the sort of interior identity that Mr. Robinson never considers." He sketched the high points of the narrative—life in Stamps, the journey to Vivian's house in St. Louis, the rape by Mr. Freeman, San Francisco, streetcars, and Marguerite's pregnancy. "[A]s she tells it," Lehmann-Haupt wrote, "what should be sad is funny, and vice versa." Angelou's blackness, he concluded, was both "absolutely essential" and "entirely irrelevant. The beauty is not in the story, but in the telling."

Newsweek's review, by Robert A. Gross, was more extensive and more effusive in its praise. "Her autobiography regularly throws out rich, dazzling images which delight and surprise with their simplicity," Gross wrote. And he went on: "But Miss Angelou's book is more than a tour de force of language or the story of childhood suffering: It quietly and gracefully portrays and pays tribute to the courage, dignity and endurance of the small, rural Southern black community in which she spent most of her early years in the 1930s."

The same issue of *Newsweek* reported on the controversy surrounding the twenty-first annual National Book Awards, which were to be held in New York on March 2, 1970. Neither Philip Roth's *Portnoy's Complaint* nor Vladimir Nabokov's *Ada* had been nominated in the fiction category (the top prize ultimately went to Joyce Carol Oates's *them*). Uncontroversially, *I Know Why the Caged Bird Sings* was nominated for an award, not in the history and biography category but in arts and letters. Angelou's book lost to Lillian Hellman's *An Unfinished Woman: A Memoir,* as did Gore Vidal's *Reflections Upon a Sinking Ship* and Richard Howard's *Alone With America.* (It's worth noting that Mary McCarthy later, famously, said of Hellman's autobiographical writings: "Every word she writes is a lie, including 'and' and 'the.'")

I Know Why the Caged Bird Sings peaked at seventh place on the *New York Times* general bestseller list, staying there for one week and remaining on the list a total of six weeks. It stayed on the *Publishers Weekly* non-fiction list for five weeks, peaking at eighth.

In November 1971, the *New York Times* reported that Angelou had been signed to direct the movie version of *I Know Why the Caged Bird*

Banned in the U.S.A.

I Know Why the Caged Bird Sings was the fourth most challenged book of 2001, according to the American Library Association's annual tabulation of attempts by people or groups to remove or restrict books in schools and libraries. Also on the list in 2000, the book was frequently cited for "sexual content, racism, offensive language, violence, and being unsuited to age group." The top three books on the list: the *Harry Potter* series by J.K. Rowling, *Of Mice and Men* by John Steinbeck, and *The Chocolate War* by Robert Cormier

Sings. But it was not until nearly eight years later, in April 1979, that a made-for-television version of the memoir was broadcast on CBS. Angelou coauthored the script with Leonora Thuna, but the movie was directed by Fielder Cook, a white TV veteran whose work includes a number of films with racial themes, among them *The Member of the Wedding* (1997) and *Judge Horton and the Scottsboro Boys* (1976).

Filmed in Vicksburg, Mississippi, the CBS film of *I Know Why the Caged Bird Sings* starred Constance Good as Maya and Diahann Carroll as her mother, Vivian. The *New York Times* called the production "a rare examination of the pain-laced joy that often accompanies growing up black and female in America." In television, Maya Angelou told the *New York Times*, "[E]veryone and his dog has a chance to pick at a writer's work. . . . Eight people sit in a room discussing characters a writer has spent nights, days, and maybe 10 bottles of sherry, developing. That's difficult for me."

In an appraisal of Angelou's body of work in *The New Yorker*, critic Hilton Als recalled that *I Know Why the Caged Bird Sings* was hailed as a new kind of memoir upon its publication. Black women who wrote about their experiences in the nineteenth and early twentieth centuries had portrayed themselves as peripheral characters in their own stories. "But Angelou took these stories public," Als wrote. "She wrote about blackness from the inside, without apology or defense."

Perhaps the best indication of the impact that *I Know Why the Caged Bird Sings* has had on American letters appears in the *New York Times Book Review*'s appraisal of the second volume of Angelou's memoir, *Gather Together in My Name*. Critic and editor Annie Gottlieb wrote, "The wisdom, rue and humor of [Angelou's] storytelling are borne on a lilting rhythm completely her own, the product of a born writer's senses nourished on black church singing and preaching, soft mother talk and salty street talk, and on literature. . . " Angelou's style, Gottlieb wrote, "has both ripened and simplified. It is more telegraphic and more condensed. . . . [I]n short, it is more like poetry." It is clear from this enthusiastic and respectful review that Angelou had become in just a few short years that which the young Marguerite / Ritie / Maya had most admired—a writer.

Other Books of Interest

Angelou's memoir was a pioneering work for countless other African-American and women writers.

○ ○ ○

I KNOW WHY THE CAGED BIRD SINGS is the first of six volumes of Maya Angelou's autobiography, all published by Random House. *Gather Together in My Name* (1974) covers the period of Angelou's life from the late 1940s to the beginnings of the civil rights movement in the late 1950s. The *Chicago Tribune* called this second volume "a gem"; the *New Yorker* said, "Miss Angelou tells the story of this dauntless, reckless, foolish girl with few flourishes; it doesn't need them."

The third volume, *Singin' and Swingin' and Gettin' Merry Like Christmas* (1976) deals with Angelou's show business career, her failed marriage to a white man, her young motherhood, and her painful relationship with the white world. The *Washington Star* found it "honest, funny, and heartwarming," praising Angelou's "lyrical writing—a god-given gift." Fourth in the series, *The Heart of a Woman* (1981) describes Angelou's life in New York City as a member of the Harlem Writers' Guild, as a coordinator of Martin Luther King's activities in the North, and as a friend of Billie Holliday and Malcolm X. Kirkus Reviews called this installment "remarkable—a great lady moving right on through a great memoir."

All God's Children Need Traveling Shoes (1986) recalls Angelou's trip to Ghana in the early 1960s. Initially undertaking the journey to enable her son to study at the University of Ghana, she ultimately experienced homesickness and a feeling of being rejected by native Africans. The

I Know Why the Caged Bird Sings

New York Times Book Review called "captivating" Angelou's "episodic engagements with a homeland that refuses to become 'home.' "

The sixth and—according to Angelou—last volume, *A Song Flung Up to Heaven* (2002), describes the assassinations of Malcolm X and Martin Luther King, the Watts riots, and her friendship with James Baldwin, who encouraged her to become a writer. Kirkus Reviews wrote: "In a nice structural turn, her autobiographical cycle ends where it began, with the first sentence of the now classic *I Know Why the Caged Bird Sings.* Alternately elegiac, meditative, and humorous, a book to savor and remember."

Angelou has also written two books of essays. *Wouldn't Take Nothing for My Journey Now* (1993) reflects on the moral and philosophical issues related to her experiences of rape, poverty, and racism. The *New York Times Book Review* said her "brief sermons on self-improvement . . . are simple but not simplistic. They are generous evidence of a life fully lived." *Even the Stars Look Lonesome* (1997) contains reflections on Africa, sex, fame, and Angelou's longtime friend and collaborator Oprah Winfrey. Kirkus Reviews commented that Angelou "again treads ballerina-like on the fine line dividing saying too much and not enough on a variety of heartfelt subjects."

Angelou has expanded her body of work with three children's books: *Life Doesn't Frighten Me* (1993), *My Painted House, My Friendly Chicken, and Me* (1994), and *Kofi and His Magic* (1996). Her numerous books of poetry include *Just Give Me a Cool Drink of Water 'fore I Diiie* (1971), *Oh Pray My Wings Are Gonna Fit Me Well* (1975), *And Still I Rise* (1978), *Now Sheba Sings the Song* (1987), *I Shall Not Be Moved* (1990), *On the Pulse of Morning* (1993), *The Completed Collected Poems of Maya Angelou* (1994), *Phenomenal Woman* (1995), and *A Brave and Startling Truth* (1995).

On top of her written works, Angelou is well known for her powerful and instantly recognizable speaking voice. Not surprisingly, there are numerous audio recordings of her reading her work. A 1957 album of her singing, *Miss Calypso,* has recently been released on compact disc. Branford Marsalis's 1994 album *Buckshot LeFonque* features a powerful track of Angelou reading Paul Laurence Dunbar's poem "Sympathy," from which she took the title of *I Know Why the Caged Bird Sings.*

The website of Wake Forest University's Z. Smith Reynolds Library cites Dolly McPherson's *Order Out of Chaos* (1990) as "the definitive work" on the writings of Maya Angelou. McPherson is a professor of English at Wake Forest and a friend of Angelou. Her book is invaluable for its addendum, "A Conversation with Maya Angelou," which includes a provocative discussion of Lillian Hellman's *An Unfinished Woman*, the book that won the National Book Award for arts and letters in 1970, defeating *I Know Why the Caged Bird Sings*. In the conversation, Angelou gives an interesting description of the process of writing a memoir about real events and real people: "I've never wanted to hurt anybody. So many of the people are still alive. The most difficult part for me has always been the selection of the incidents. To find one which is dramatic without being melodramatic or maudlin, and yet will give me that chance to show that aspect of human personality, of life, which impacted on me from which I drew and grew."

BY OTHER AUTHORS

An attempt to list works by African-American writers only scratches the surface of a robust field. Some selected titles follow.

BLACK BOY
by Richard Wright (Harper, 1945)
Considered among Wright's greatest works, this autobiographical novel chronicles Wright's journey from a harsh boyhood in Mississippi in the early twentieth century to the political and literary world of Chicago in the 1930s. Along the way, Wright struggles both with stinging racism from whites in the South (and the North) and with fellow blacks who are unable or unwilling to accept his individuality and his literary ambitions.

THE BONDWOMAN'S NARRATIVE
by Hannah Crafts (Time Warner, 2002)
Prominent black scholar Henry Louis Gates discovered this manuscript while browsing through an auction catalog in 2001. After confirming its authenticity through exhaustive research, Gates asserted that *The Bondwoman's Narrative* was written in the 1850s and was likely the first novel ever written by an African-American woman. Crafts's sometimes sentimental but always gripping autobiographical tale tells of her escape from slavery in the South and the obstacles she faces along the road to freedom.

FROM SLAVERY TO FREEDOM: A HISTORY OF AFRICAN AMERICANS
   by John Hope Franklin and Alfred A. Moss (Knopf, 2000)
Originally published in 1947, Franklin and Moss's volume has long been
considered the definitive history of the African-American experience.
The authors trace America's black population from origins in Africa
through the slave trade, the Civil War, and Reconstruction. *From Slavery
to Freedom* also looks at African-American cultural contributions, most
notably the Harlem Renaissance of the 1920s.

MAKES ME WANNA HOLLER
   by Nathan McCall (Random House, 1994)
This riveting autobiography looks at the experience of growing up as a
young black man in urban America. McCall, now a reporter for the
Washington Post, recounts his journey from gang-dominated childhood
streets to a stint in prison and finally to a successful career as a journalist.
McCall's inspiring and honest portrayal of his missteps and his ultimately
fulfilling search for role models has made *Makes Me Wanna Holler* one
of the most lauded autobiographies of recent years.

THE COLLECTED POEMS OF LANGSTON HUGHES
   edited by Arnold Rampersad and David Roessel (Vintage, 1995)
Among the poets, writers, and other artists traditionally associated with
the Harlem Renaissance, Hughes was regarded as a leader, a man with a
clear vision for the role of black artists in America. Though he wrote in
many genres, Hughes is perhaps best known for his poems, in which he
experimented with form and rhythm and made an effort to incorporate
elements of African-American music, especially jazz.